SAMSKARA

by Lanre Malaolu

Samskara was commissioned by The Yard Theatre, with support from Arts Council England, Jerwood Arts New Work Fund, Battersea Arts Centre and The Society for Theatre Research. Supporting partner East London Dance.

Samskara was first performed at The Yard, London, on 8 November 2021

SAMSKARA
Lanre Malaolu

Cast

Silent Man	Paaliba Abugre
Wisdom	Oliver Alvin-Wilson
Father	Will Atiomo
Young Buck	Ntonga Mwanza
Older	Razak Osman
Drummer	Yahael Camara Onono

Creative Team

Writer, Director & Choreographer	Lanre Malaolu
Assistant Choreographer	Rochea Dyer
Assistant Director	Kirk-Ann Roberts
Dramaturg	Anthony Simpson-Pike
Technical Stage & Production Manager	Meg Hodgson
Associate Designer	Natalie Pryce
Lighting Designer	Ali Hunter
Composer & Sound Designer	Jan Baranowski
Additional Composition	Yahael Camara Onono
Creative Producer	Shereen Hamilton
Executive Producer	Ruby Baker

Cast and Creative Team

Lanre Malaolu (*Writer, Director & Choreographer*)
Lanre is a director, choreographer and writer working across theatre and film. He creates work that seamlessly intertwines movement and dialogue to tell socially engaged stories about our world. In 2019, he was commissioned by the Camden People's Theatre to present his semi-autobiographical solo show *Elephant in the Room*, which later transferred to the Roundhouse Theatre, London. Lanre's hybrid dance-documentary film *The Circle* had its world premiere at Sheffield Doc/Fest. It was acquired by the *Guardian* in 2020 and streamed on their online platforms. He was the choreographer and performer for the British Council commissioned film *Dear Mr Shakespeare*, which was featured at Sundance Film Festival 2017. His film *The Conversation* was selected for the BAFTA-recognised Aesthetica Film Festival, winning the Best Dance Film Award in 2020. He also won the Best Director award at S.O.U.L. Festival (supported by BFI and The British Blacklist, 2021). Movement direction credits include *Pass Over* (Kiln Theatre) for which Lanre was nominated for Best Choreographer at the Black British Theatre Awards in 2020, *Blue/Orange* (Birmingham Rep), *Othello* (English Touring Theatre) and *So Many Reasons* (Soho Theatre). Lanre trained at Drama Centre London and has worked extensively as an actor, performing at venues including the Royal Shakespeare Company, the Royal Court and Shakespeare's Globe, as well as in a number of screen roles. Lanre is currently developing his first feature with BBC Film.

Paaliba Abugre (*Silent Man*)
Paaliba Abugre began his training in Swansea with Groundswell Dance Company first beginning in the street-dance styles. He later expanded his range with contemporary, ballet and jazz dance before moving to London to train at The Urdang Academy. Paaliba continuously strives to merge all that he's learned, in and out of dance, to create a versatile, aesthetic and artistic form of expression. Previous credits include *Heartbeat of Home* (Europe and Asia tour), *West End Live*, *River Dream*, John McColgan, Assistant Choreographer, Fila Disruptor, Guerilla Creative, Melody Squire, Turning Tides Festival, The Rise Collective, Mahla Axon.

Oliver Alvin-Wilson (*Wisdom*)
Oliver Alvin-Wilson's theatre credits include *All of Us, The Red Barn* and *All's Well That Ends Well* (National Theatre), *Nine Night* (National Theatre and Trafalgar Studios), *The Doctor* (Almeida Theatre*), The Twilight Zone* (Almeida Theatre and the Ambassadors Theatre), *A Midsummer Night's Dream* (Young Vic), *The Gala* (RSC) and *Genesis Inc.* (Hampstead Theatre). Olivier has also worked with Propeller Theatre Company, Stafford Gatehouse Theatre, Pilot Theatre, Leeds Playhouse, Nuffield Theatre and Theatr Clwyd. His television and film work includes *Wonder Woman 1984* (DC Entertainment/Warner Bros), *The Huntsman* (Universal Pictures), *The Bay* and *From Cradle to Grave* (ITV), *Collateral* (BBC), *Lovesick* (Netflix), *The Rebel – Series 2* (UK TV Gold) and *Misfits* (Clerkenwell Films/Channel 4).

Will Atiomo (*Father*)
Will Atiomo is an actor from Nottingham. He recently trained with the National Youth Theatre Rep Company. He will make his screen debut in Netflix's *The Sandman*, released 2022. Theatre credits include *Animal Farm* (directed by Ed Stambollouian), *Othello* (Miranda Cromwell), *Ordinary Miracle* (Marsha Kevinovna), all for the National Youth Theatre Rep Company.

Ntonga Mwanza (*Young Buck*)
Born and raised in Zambia and now residing in London, Ntonga Mwanza is an actor, writer and dancer. Ntonga made his debut in first feature film *Leave2remain* with award-winning director Bruce Goodison, he then starred in *Doctors* (BBC), Channel 4 series *Babylon* directed by Danny Boyle, *Hotel* directed by Maria Aberg at the National Theatre, the lead in *The Meet-Up* at the Royal Court and the lead role in feature film *Honey Trap* by director Rebecca Johnson, which received four stars in the *Guardian*, and is currently available to watch on Netflix. Ntonga studied BTEC Performing Arts at Leyton Sixth-Form College where he graduated with three Distinctions. He then studied Dance Performance at Middlesex University and went on to pursue his acting career full time at The Identity School of Acting. Whilst maintaining his

training he then joined/performed with Avante Garde Dance Company (*Breaking Convention*, Sadler Wells) and Definitives (*Breaking Convention/World of Dance*, France and Germany) where he gained his skills and techniques in hip-hop breakdance and intuitive storytelling movement. He also recently toured his one-man show *Resonate*, produced by Nouveau Riche (award-winning plays *Queens of Sheba/Typical*) with English Touring Theatre and Paines Plough Brixton. He first performed his self-written play at the Omnibus Theatre Engine Room Take Over in 2018, and then at the VAULT Festival in 2019, and is now currently developing his second play.

Razak Osman (*Older*)

Razak Osman is an artist from East London. He trained as an actor at ArtsEd, and since graduating he's been featured in the TV series *You, Me and The Apocalypse*, Studio 3 Arts, *Merchant of Venice*, Olivier Award-winning opera *Katya Kabanova* at the Royal Opera House, *Wolf of Wall Street: The Immersive Play*, *No Strings Attached* at the King's Head Theatre, and many other productions. He also trained for many years as a dancer at various studios across London in the street-dance styles, hip-hop, popping and house. He's been featured in various music videos, and has taught at Pineapple Studios. He performed with Olivier Award-winning dance company BoyBlue Ent, at Sadler's Wells and the Barbican. In his free time, Razak loves longboarding around London, cycling, training in the martial art Brazilian jiu-jitsu, live streaming himself DJing his favourite tunes from his living room, and teaching himself new things. He'd love to be able to speak French and Spanish – will he ever learn, who knows?

Yahael Camara Onono (*Drummer*)

Yahael Camara Onono was born in North-West London to Nigerian and Senegalese parents. Despite being born in the UK and growing up in inner city London for most of his life, he had an affinity for his folkloric music from a very young age. He received his first talking drum at the age of six from his grandfather, and later started playing the djembe at the age of eight. Though he grew up in Harlesden, he was given the gift of an open mind through travel at an early age. He has since gone on to play with and accompanied many groups, bands and ensembles including Family Atlantica, Maisha, the composers Burna Boy and Wande Coal just to name a few. He is most known, however, for his role as Musical Director and Band Leader of Balimaya Project, a sixteen-piece collective in London that intently infuses traditional mande music with jazz and other styles in the diaspora to create a unique sound and also a renaissance within the culture, making traditional folkloric music styles more accessible. Their debut album is out now and is taking the jazz scene by storm!

Rochea Dyer (*Assistant Choreographer*)
Rochea Dyer is an interdisciplinary artist, choreographer and teacher specialising in the combination of art forms such as movement, physical theatre and spoken word. Rochea's aim is to create performance work that triggers deeper thinking by exploring themes that should not be ignored or overlooked in society. At the heart of her work is the intimacy of that spectator/performer relationship and how that connection enhances performance art to a higher level. She has gone from touring at the Edinburgh Festival Fringe and working in the West End on shows such as *Breaking Convention* and *Into the Hoods* by Kate Prince. To working as an assistant choreographer for the award-winning actor Regé Jean-Page's music video 'Don't Wait'. In addition to short award-winning films such as *The Conversation* by Lanre Malaolu, winning Best Dance Film at BAFTA-recognised Aesthetica Film Festival and San Francisco Dance Film Festival, 2020. The driving force behind Rochea's passion is the art of making revolutionary work.

Kirk-Ann Roberts (*Assistant Director*)
Kirk-Ann Roberts is a Caribbean-born, London-based, spoken-word poet, playwright and theatre director. Inspired by movement and visual art, her work often focuses on identity and the human experience. She is a Roundhouse Resident Artist and a graduate of Young Vic's Director Programme. A workshop facilitator and creative practitioner, she has worked for the likes of Talawa Theatre, Emergency Exit Arts and The London Bubble.

Anthony Simpson-Pike (*Dramaturg*)
Anthony Simpson-Pike is a director, dramaturg and writer whose work has been staged in theatres including the Bush, the Gate, the Young Vic and the Royal Court. He is currently Associate Director at The Yard Theatre, was previously Resident Director at Theatre Peckham and Associate Director at The Gate Theatre. Anthony is also a facilitator, having worked with young people and communities at the Gate, the Royal Court, the Young Vic, Shakespeare's Globe and the National Theatre. Recent directorial

work includes *Lava* by Benedict Lombe (Bush Theatre), *Living Newspaper* (Royal Court), *The Electric* by Vickie Donoghue (Paines Plough/ RWCMD), and *The Ridiculous Darkness* by Wolfram Lotz (Gate Theatre). As a dramaturg, Anthony has developed multiple seasons of work for the Gate and The Yard as Associate Director. Recent dramaturgical credits include *Hotline* with Produced Moon (Tron Theatre), *Dear Young Monster* by Pete McHale (The Queer House), and *Coup de Grace* by Almudena Ramirez (Royal Court). Anthony is also a reader for the Royal Court.

Meg Hodgson (*Technical Stage & Production Manager*)
Meg Hodgson is a technical production/stage manager and lighting designer who also has their own performance practice. They've worked with artists such as Stacy Makishi and Le Gateau Chocolat and are currently in the process of making their first full-length solo show *Moonface*.

Natalie Pryce (*Associate Designer*)
Theatre includes *Red Velvet* at RADA, *846 Live* at Theatre Royal Stratford East, *Me for the World* at the Young Vic, *Ducklings* at the Royal Exchange, (Co -Set and Costume Designer), *For All the Women Who Thought They Were Mad* at Hackney Showroom, *Not Now, Bernard* at the Unicorn. As Costume Designer, theatre includes *Old Bridge* (Papatango Theatre Company/Bush), *White Noise* (Bridge), *Is God Is* (Royal Court), *Anna X* (West End), *Tales of the Turntable* (Zoonation), and (as Costume Supervisor) *The Winter's Tale* at Shakespeare's Globe. As Costume Designer, film includes *Good Grief*, *Fourteen Fractures*, *Myrtle*, *Fellow Creatures*, *Swept Under Rug* and (as Costume Trainee) *My Name is Leon*.

Ali Hunter (*Lighting Designer*)
Ali is a freelance lighting designer working in dance, theatre and opera. She was the Young Associate Lighting Designer for Matthew Bourne's *Romeo and Juliet* in 2019. Other recent lighting-design credits include: Dance: *Inscribed in 'Me'* (Alethia Antonia), *Happy Father's Day* (Dani Harris Walters), *Vital Stages* (Studio 3 Arts), *Benched* (Leila McMillan), *The Quake Within* (Yun Cheng), *Deuce* (Iona Brie), *Foreign Body* (Southbank Centre for WOW). Theatre: *Small Change* (Clapham Omnibus), *Brief Encounter* (The Watermill), *Fix* (Pleasance Islington), *The Man Who Wanted to Be a Penguin* (Stuff and Nonsense), *Mother of Him* (Park 200), *For Services Rendered, The Play About My Dad, Woman Before a Glass* (Jermyn Street), *Cash Cow* (Hampstead), *Muckers* (The Egg, Conde Duque, Oxford Playhouse), *Soft Animals* (Soho), *Sugar, Don't Forget the Birds*, *Rattlesnake* (Open Clasp),

Clear White Light (Live Theatre Newcastle), *Fairytale Revolution, Out of Sorts, Isaac Came Home from the Mountain, Cinderella and the Beanstalk* (Theatre503). Opera: *La Nonne Sanglante* (Gothic Opera), *Treemonisha*, *The Boatswain's Mate* (Spectra), *Gracie, The Biograph Girl* (Finborough), *Tenderly* (New Wimbledon Studio), *Katzenmusik* (Royal Court). As Associate Lighting Designer: *Hot Mess* (Candoco Dance), *The Half God of Rainfall* (Birmingham Rep and Kiln, lighting designer: Jackie Shemesh).

Jan Baranowski *(Sound Designer)*
Jan Baranowski is a composer, sound designer, engineer and pianist pioneering at the forefront of electronic music. Having played piano as a child, Jan left Warsaw at the age of eighteen and moved to London to study a degree in jazz and pursue a music career. Film work includes short films such as *The Circle* (longlist candidate for BAFTA Best British Short Film and winner of the Parliamentary Award Film The House). *The Circle* was officially released online via the *Guardian* in 2020. Jan has also scored *The Conversation* (Best Dance Film Winner at Aesthetica Film Festival). Jan's body of work includes scores and sound design for theatre pieces such as Saskia Horton's *Life According to Motown*, which received The Place Startin' Point Comission, and Lanre Malaolu's sold-out solo show *Elephant in the Room*. Jan is also an assistant engineer at 5 dB, a project based in West London that helps young, talented and underprivileged musicians produce and record their music at a world-class level.

Shereen Hamilton *(Creative Producer)*
Shereen is a dedicated and versatile creative practitioner. Alongside her BA and MA in Theatre and Performance, specialising in the intersectionality of race and gender in theatrical representations, Shereen has trained and worked as a producer, director, actor, stage manager and facilitator. Her area of work centres around intersectional identities on stage, current and historical politic, theatre as a vehicle of education and diversifying the theatre we see today. After being Project Manager for the *Samskara* R&D and Lanre Malaolu's *Elephant in the Room* at the Roundhouse in 2019, Shereen was selected as part of The Roundhouse Future Producers 2020. Prior to this, Shereen has worked as Assistant Producer on *Evolution Festival* at the Lyric Hammersmith and has produced and directed *Bitchcraft,* part of Melanin Box Festival at Theatre Peckham and then to Blacktress UK, part of the John Thaw Initiative. Shereen's recent directing credits include assistant directing *seven methods of killing kylie jenner* at the Royal Court in 2019 and 2021 and directing *CRIPtic Pit Party* at the Barbican in 2019.

Shereen has undergone training with Talawa on Creating Routes 2019 and with Company Three on Making Theatre with Young People, resulting in her becoming one of Company Three's Young Peoples Facilitators.

Ruby Baker (*Executive Producer*)
As a creative producer, Ruby works across art forms and disciplines to reimagine spaces and challenge traditional presentation methods. Her background in outdoor arts and festivals means Ruby often works in unconventional environments, a practice that is combined with a commitment to championing underrepresented art forms. Ruby splits her time as a freelancer and as Senior Creative Producer at Poet in the City and is also the Creative Director for Cloud9 Festival. Prior to this, Ruby led the artist development and professional performance programmes for East London Dance. Ruby has worked as a creative producer for *East Wall* at Tower of London, listed as the *Guardian*'s 'Top 25 Dance Productions of the 21st Century', *Equality Always Fits*, *A Celebration of Pride* with Levi's UK® and *Identity*, a co-production with Shoreditch Town Hall. Previous collaborations include London College of Fashion, Coventry City of Culture, Emergency Exit Arts, Feminist Review, London Mela, Latitude Festival, Mahogany Carnival Company, the National Theatre and Latitude Festival.

The Yard Theatre

'*The future has arrived in Hackney Wick in the form of The Yard*'
Lyn Gardner, *Guardian*

The Yard is a theatre and music venue in a converted warehouse in Hackney Wick.

The Yard was founded by Artistic Director Jay Miller in 2011, with support from Tarek Iskander, Sasha Milavic Davies and Alex Rennie and a group of fifty volunteers. They worked with architectural firm Practice Architecture to convert a disused warehouse into a theatre and bar.

The Yard is at the centre of its community, reaching thousands of local people every year through programmes in local schools and in the community centres they run: Hub67 in Hackney Wick and The Hall in East Village. They run creative projects for young people aged 4–19 years to make work for their stage, and offer regular activities and resources for local people.

The Yard is also one of London's most exciting venues for experiencing music, welcoming parties by and for under-represented groups in London's music scene, as well as hosting internationally renowned DJs and promoters every weekend. Since 2011 The Yard's work has been seen by hundreds of thousands of people and shows have transferred to the National Theatre, been turned into television series and toured the UK.

The Yard Theatre

SAMSKARA

Lanre Malaolu

The Black Nod is not just 'hey, racism exists and we've got a coherent experience…', The Black Nod between mandem is also, sorry we was all such dickheads to each other fam…

Akala

So did you see who shot you?

yes I saw his touch
its pulse like my father
who held me twice
the day I was born
the day I angered him

Caleb Femi, 'Repress'

Author's Note

I'd like to thank a few people who've helped to build, develop and plant the seeds for *Samskara* over the last decade. Some of these people are aware of this, some aren't.

Thank you to the brothers at HMP Thameside in 2016, for being vulnerable with me during those six weeks of workshops, in an environment that doesn't promote vulnerability in any way, shape or form.

Thank you to my incredible cast, creative team and The Yard for your continuous work, passion and engagement during (and after) rehearsals. You're all Gs.

Thank you to Valentine Olukoga. The bravery and heart you showed me and the cast within those three days will stay with me for the rest of my life.

Thank you to Derek Owusu. *Safe* was the first book I read where I truly felt seen.

Finally, they say your greatest challenges are your greatest teachers. So, thank you, Dad. I wouldn't have created *Samskara* without having the experience I did growing up.

L.M., 2021

Characters

YOUNG BUCK
OLDER
FATHER
WISDOM
SILENT MAN
DRUMMER

Setting

A row of four chairs upstage-centre, where the ensemble will sit.

A chair on the outskirts of the space, where DRUMMER will sit.

A Few Notes

Words in **bold** in a character's line denote where movement could perhaps happen, either as the word is *spoken*, or to *replace* the words.

A triple dash (---) denotes where movement could perhaps happen between words.

Unless stated otherwise, lines spoken by characters who are not directly involved in the scene are to be delivered from their seated position.

Unless stated otherwise, characters are to directly address the audience with all dialogue.

All movement sequences and stage directions are a template. The performers and collaborators will use this as a base to work from. Many ideas may stay, many may go.

I wouldn't call this a play.

I also wouldn't call this a dance show.

This text went to press before the end of rehearsals and so may differ slightly from the play as performed.

Prologue

The following action will happen as the audience enters the auditorium…

SILENT MAN *paces up and down the space. Deeply focused, but slightly apprehensive.*

DRUMMER *enters the space, cracks his hands and neck – stretches out, preparing. Sits behind his drum on the outskirts of the space – continues his preparations.*

SILENT MAN *stops centre-stage. Looks out at the people entering, moving between seats, the people sat… Then shoots off again. He's psyching himself up for an intense challenge ahead. This will happen a few more times until the audience are all in. At which point,* SILENT MAN *lands centre-stage and looks out to the audience for a beat. He takes a deep breath in and… exhales.*

Beat.

He turns to DRUMMER, *gives him a nod.* DRUMMER *nods back, then begins hitting his drum. As soon as he does,* SILENT MAN *runs offstage.*

Beat.

He returns, dragging two large heavy sacks. Drops them centre-stage, opens one, reaches in and lifts out fresh, moist soil. He looks at it for a moment, squeezes it, meaningfully, then shoots to the outskirts of the space and begins to pepper the soil around it. This should be done as a sacred ritual. The more soil that is laid, the faster and more intense the drumming gets.

We eventually see that SILENT MAN *is creating a large semicircle with the soil.*

SILENT MAN *finishes. He stands, breathless. Looks at his hands and slowly wipes them on his T-shirt.*

Beat.

*He takes a breath in and begins a repetitive movement motif.
The energy of it feels like a calling of some kind.*

Beat.

YOUNG BUCK *jolts into the space. He looks around, pissed
off and confused. He suddenly clocks the threshold of soil at his
feet, then looks up at* SILENT MAN. *He crosses over the soil,
wants to figure out what the hell* SILENT MAN *is doing.*

Beat.

OLDER *jolts into the space. He looks around and then looks at*
SILENT MAN, *intrigued. He crosses the threshold and, as soon
as he does,* YOUNG BUCK *turns and clocks* OLDER, *registers
him as a threat.*

Beat.

OLDER *gives* YOUNG BUCK *a nod… The Black Man's Nod.*
YOUNG BUCK *responds with the smallest of nods back, then
looks back to* SILENT MAN.

OLDER *inspects the space, perhaps he grabs a handful of soil,
plays with it between his fingers.*

YOUNG BUCK *walks closer to* SILENT MAN. *He smirks,
then mockingly does* SILENT MAN's *motif.* SILENT MAN
ignores him. His focus will not waver…

FATHER *jolts into the space. He stands behind the threshold of
soil, sombre, but a look in his eyes, as if he was expecting to be
here. He takes a breath, then crosses over. As soon as he does,*
YOUNG BUCK *and* OLDER *acknowledge his presence.
Another tense moment between the men, which simmers down
with a couple of head nods.*

SILENT MAN's *motif builds…*

A pensive WISDOM *slowly enters the space – on guard and
fully in control.*

*He stands behind the threshold for a very long moment, then
takes the smallest of steps over the threshold into the circle. But
he doesn't move from his spot, just canvasses the space with his
proud stance. Again, the men register* WISDOM. *He eyes them
back. Then, after a beat, changes his mind and turns to leave…*

Meanwhile, SILENT MAN*'s motif and the drumming reach a crescendo into…*

Silence.

WISDOM *stops and turns back.*

SILENT MAN *turns to the men, breathless. He sees the men for the first time and takes this moment in.*

Beat.

SILENT MAN *suddenly takes a sharp breath in. After a beat, a readied* FATHER *does the same. An intrigued* OLDER *follows.* WISDOM, *still tense, kind of wants to see where this goes, he takes a breath in.*

All that's left is YOUNG BUCK. *He looks at them as if they're all crazy people. Maybe has a little chuckle to himself, then mockingly takes a sharp breath in and…*

SLAM!

DRUMMER *hits the drum and the men explode into the space, taking us into…*

'Keep It Tight and Keep Going'

Our first collective movement sequence, underscored by
DRUMMER.

*During this, we will see fragments of what these men hold…
their pain.*

*We'll also see moments of collective joy, as well as the
unspoken, yet universal, interpersonal black male physicality.*

The sequence crescendos with the ensemble and SILENT MAN
*marching together, in sync. They start to move backwards
towards the seats, while* SILENT MAN *goes towards the
outskirts of the space. He's still within the circle of soil, but
closer to* DRUMMER. *He sits on the floor.*

The rest of the ensemble sit on the chairs, taking us into…

'Why Is Your Leg Touching Me Fam?!'

*The men are pretty up-close, arms touching and whatnot. After
a beat,* YOUNG BUCK *shifts, nudging* FATHER*'s leg, which
slightly touches his. This could be so subtle we think it's just the
performer shifting.*

FATHER *shifts position, trying to create more space for himself
and nudges* YOUNG BUCK *by accident (on purpose…) along
the way.*

This builds and builds as FATHER *and* YOUNG BUCK *try to
physically top the other to create more space for themselves.
Opening legs wider, stretching arms across, etc. Light and
humorous.*

*The other characters notice the commotion every now and then,
but other than that, continue to look out.*

The sequence crescendos and we have a winner…

FATHER, *who's outdone* YOUNG BUCK *by standing on the chair in some crazy-ass way, or something. A pissed* YOUNG BUCK *shoots up and into the space.*

SILENT MAN *eyes him, then begins a movement motif, one that feels and looks like a personalised calling for* YOUNG BUCK.

YOUNG BUCK *looks at* SILENT MAN, *confused, but nonetheless he starts to do it with him, with a smile. Still taking this whole thing as a joke. He repeats the motif in rhythm with 'You see me…'*

YOUNG BUCK. **You see me** yeah!… **You see me!…**

SILENT MAN *suddenly does a movement with his arms towards* YOUNG BUCK, *which whips him towards the audience and straight into –*

You see me?!… I can do what I want! I can do what I want, when I want and no one can tell me nuffin! I'm the boss man, captain, commander, CEO, officer!!!… But obviously, I ain't no fed. If I was in a boy band yeah? If I was in a boy band!…

YOUNG BUCK *looks back to the chairs, as if calling on the men.* OLDER *and* FATHER *rise from their seats and approach the left and right flank of* YOUNG BUCK, *creating a boy-band trio. Lights change and the men snap into some kind of Boyz II Men dance routine (with relevant music!). Over this…*

I'd be the one in the middle. You know, the main one that the other two are always looking at onstage – make sure they're getting the moves right and lyrics on point. Yeah, that's me, the one in the middle.

OLDER *and* FATHER *peel back to their seats.*

Top boy! Big cheese!! Even in school, everyone knows! Except for this one teacher…

YOUNG BUCK *does a movement. This could be something subtle… a click, perhaps, or the opposite, something more overt as a clear calling. In either case, it initiates* OLDER *to stand and he begins to physicalise 'Mr Ogun'.*

Mr Ogun... the semi-professional wasteman. Semi, 'cause he's so shit at everything he does, man can't even be the full-professional wasteman!... Wasteman. On my ass every day, handing me detention cards like free McDonald's vouchers! And this man's hands were DRYYYY! Swear down, if you looked at his hands without seeing his face, you legit would have thought dis brudda was white. The way he just didn't like me! Always used to give me this look, with those eyes...

I mean, yeah, I might roll to class late a couple times, might be on my phone in assembly, might slap up a Year 9 for chatting gas, but so what! I ain't the only one. He's always tryna tell me what to do, and no one tells me what to do! Except my dad innit... But he ain't here now, so no one can tell me nuffin! YO! There was this one time in school...

FATHER *shoots up from his seat, he has a childlike energy about him.*

A bunch of us were huddled together at lunchtime –

FATHER. Your mum's so stupid, she stared at a carton of apple juice for twelve hours 'cause it said 'concentrate'!!

YOUNG BUCK. Fat Ivan was doing one of his 'your mum' runs –

FATHER. Your mum's so old, she knew Burger King when he was a prince!!

YOUNG BUCK. Picking random people and just grilling them –

FATHER. Your mum's so fat, she can't even jump to a conclusion!!

YOUNG BUCK. Man had a collection –

FATHER (*looking at* YOUNG BUCK). Your mum's so ugly when she tried to join an ugly contest, they said... 'Sorry, no professionals!!'

YOUNG BUCK. WHAT?!

FATHER. Nah nah nah, I didn't mean to look at you fam!! I was –

YOUNG BUCK *suddenly swipes his hand, as if slapping someone* – DRUMMER *simultaneously hits the drum.*

FATHER *suddenly holds his face, in pain.*

YOUNG BUCK. No one talks about my mum like that, not even on a gas ting. And I'm there just like –

YOUNG BUCK *swipes his hand multiple times* – DRUMMER *slaps the drum on each swipe.* FATHER *reacts.*

I dunno what it is about bitch-slapping someone that feels so good! But the slaps got Mr Ogun's spider senses tingling and he flew out on a mad one –

FATHER *sits.* OLDER *shoots up.*

OLDER. BREAK IT UP RIGHT NOW!!

YOUNG BUCK. Everyone split like some wussies! Me? Taking my sweet time! Cah I notice my laces are undone innit and obviously, man don't wanna trip up and buss my lip! Best believe I got a line of girls who won't be too happy about that! Gotta keep the merchandise pristine, get me! Plus… I wanted to make sure I did it properly innit. Dad always used to say –

WISDOM *stands.*

WISDOM. If you're gonna do something, make sure you do it properly.

YOUNG BUCK. And this semi-professional wasteman comes breezing towards me, arms flailing about, blowing the shit out of his whistle and –

OLDER. MY OFFICE, NOOOOOW!!!!

YOUNG BUCK. Do teachers go on a course on how to make their voice as loud as possible when they shout? 'Cause it's not like a normal shout, it's bare deep and got this echo to it… Two-twos, I'm in his office now, and he's there chillin, laying back on his chair, crusty hands crossed and he just looks at me. Doesn't say a word, just looks at me, dead in the eye. But the way he looks at me… he can't look at me like that, he don't get to… my dad looked at me like that, when I did something wrong. Felt like Superman laser-eyes going through my skull – and this semi-professional wasteman is still looking at me! Inside, I'm shouting 'Stop!' Outside? Calm. Just do the same…

YOUNG BUCK *stares ahead for a beat.*

Then he starts smiling, so…

YOUNG BUCK *flashes his pearly whites.*

OLDER. I feel sorry for your mum. Keep going down this route, and you will end up dead or in prison. Mark my words.

YOUNG BUCK*'s smile fades.* SILENT MAN *leans forwards, watching him intently. Perhaps on the following words in bold he physically echoes the same movement* YOUNG BUCK *does.*

YOUNG BUCK. And he wouldn't stop looking at me… the way he was… he was tryna make me feel like I'm beneath him. A grain of sand, a number on a sheet – looking at me like I'm a dog --- like I'm a dog with no bark --- like I'm a dog with no bark, when the bark is all I know, like I'm too slow – like I'm always **too slow** – like I can't do anything right – looking at me like there's nothing left. Like he knows what goes on in my **head** – like he *thinks* he knows – like he can see the **thoughts** – feel the **heaviness** – hear the **whispers** – like I'm a cheat, a fake, an empty shell – looking at me like I'm a --- I'm a ---

YOUNG BUCK*'s movement builds into a repetitive motif – tumbles out of control, until it reaches a crescendo and he suddenly snaps out of it, into…*

WHAT I'M SAYING IS… HE'S LOOKING AT ME LIKE I'M A SEMI-PROFESSIONAL WASTEMAN!!!!… wasteman.

SILENT MAN *stands and walks up to* YOUNG BUCK. *They hold eye contact for a beat. Seems like a stand-off from* YOUNG BUCK*'s perspective.* SILENT MAN *takes a* *breath, then begins a motif towards* YOUNG BUCK, *but before he can fully physicalise it,* YOUNG BUCK *laughs at him and bops back to his seat.*

Beat.

SILENT MAN *feels the failure of his attempt. He looks out to the audience.*

Lights change. An empty spotlight downstage-centre, perhaps. After a beat, SILENT MAN *bops into it, then leaves.*

After a beat, he bops into it again, but this time? The bop has a bit more BOP to it. Nope... still doesn't feel right... he stops, rewinds the bop, starts again...

This will go on a few more times, as he tries to perfect his 'Black Man Bop' (the audience essentially being his bedroom mirror). He may trip over himself at times, as well as a heap of other moments to be found. This sequence will be light and comical to the outside eye, but he will be taking it DEADLY seriously.

After a few moments, he gives up, frustrated. He turns towards OLDER *and begins a motif – a personalised calling for him.* OLDER *stands, starts to pick the movement up. As he does, he repeats it in rhythm of the words 'I wanna feel...' below.*

OLDER. **I wanna feel... I wanna feel...**

SILENT MAN *suddenly does a movement with his arms towards* OLDER, *which whips him towards the audience and straight into –*

I wanna feel that old-school hip hop and R&B vibrating through my chest. I'm talking Blackstreet, B.I.G., Jodeci, Usher... *Confessions* album only. I wanna feel it permeating my bones taking me to that higher place, that sacred place, that feeling...

That feeling when you're in a club with your boys and the banging track of the month comes on! There was this one time, I was in this club in Dalston and the DJ kept pulling up

Sisqó's 'Thong Song'… it was a madness! Man had the whole club singing 'Let me see that thong!' for thirty minutes, straight! That feeling of dancing the way you wanna dance, that freedom. But it's all about the DJ. A good DJ would play tracks like 'Thong Song' or Ludacris' 'Stand Up', which they knew would get the club hype all night. But a great DJ knows you can't sustain that! So they might drop in some Drake to chop it up a bit… toilet break… drink top-up. But there's one song that they'd always play at peak clubbing time. When the inside of the windows are steamed up and inhibitions are on the other side of them, when there's as much sweat pouring as there is alcohol. 'Cause they know the unwritten rule. You can only play it once a night. 'Cause when they do, and you happen to be black… YOU. DROP. EVERYTHING. It is not a drill, it's life or death! Even the mandem chained to the back walls, bottles in hand join in! Because it is a Black Call to Action…

During the last few lines, 'Candy' by Cameo fades in. The ensemble instinctively lift their heads, like lions smelling the scent of a kill. They rise and step towards OLDER…

SILENT MAN *joins them…*

Once together, 'Candy' fully blares out from the speakers and you know what happens next…!!!

The energy, happiness and freedom is palpable. All because of these simple steps they do together.

After a couple of rounds, OLDER *steps forwards. The music simmers down and underscores the following…*

And you have this feeling… this unspoken bond. In that moment we're together, one, in sync… except for that awkward white brudda at the back, who keeps tripping over his feet, or needs to be taught again and again…

YOUNG BUCK/FATHER/WISDOM. And again…

OLDER. But us? We're vibsing, laughing, rhythmically floating in that stereotype and we don't give a damn! You can't buy that, you know? It's always there… but sometimes it's hard to find.

SILENT MAN *walks up to* OLDER. *They hold eye contact for a moment.* SILENT MAN *takes a breath, then begins a motif… the one he attempted with* YOUNG BUCK, *but now, we see it play out fully for the first time. He's doing a kind of pulling motif towards* OLDER*'s chest, as if pulling some invisible yet visceral thing out of him.*

OLDER *stands, unmoved. He glares at his chest, then back to* SILENT MAN.

Beat.

OLDER *strolls back to his seat, the world on his shoulders and unable to shake it off.*

SILENT MAN *is alone again. There is a spotlight, downstage-centre.*

SILENT MAN *enters it and immediately starts to nod his head at the audience. Then stops, tries again, but on a different angle and with different energy… Nope, still doesn't feel right. Tries something else – chin a bit higher maybe? – nope – lower? – Yeah, lower – hmmm – side-angle head nod? Nah – nope – less, do less…*

Essentially, we watch as he tries to perfect The Black Man Nod as best as he can. Again, he's taking it DEADLY seriously, but this should come across light and comical. After a few moments, he gives up, annoyed at himself.

Lights fade up. SILENT MAN *looks towards* FATHER *and begins a motif – a personalised calling for* FATHER *and* FATHER *alone.* FATHER *starts to pick it up and stands. He repeats the motif in rhythm with his words 'I remember…'*

FATHER. **I remember… I remember…**

SILENT MAN *suddenly does a movement with his arms towards* FATHER, *which whips him towards the audience and straight into –*

I remember the moment he first arrived. I remember thinking, how do women do it?! A whole damn thing, coming out of their… The way the big man upstairs gave us bruthas a free pass! But for some reason, he skipped over sea horses… it

was a few weeks before his due date, and I was watching this *National Geographic* documentary. Did you know that in the sea kingdom, male sea horses are the ones who give birth?! They court the female, she transfers her eggs into his pouch thing and a few weeks later, the brutha gives birth!! MAD! And it must have lodged in my mind – 'cause
I had this dream, this weird… you know how sometimes in dreams you could be looking at someone who starts off as one person, then suddenly transforms into someone else?… Well, that's what happened in this dream, but the thing is… I was the one who transformed. Man went from a whole six-foot-three black man… to a two-inch sea horse.

And not only am I a sea horse, but I'm in a bed now! And it's all blurry and I'm blinking, tryna make out the room, tryna get my bearings… I look to my left and make out a tray of scalpels, scissors, gloves… I'm in a hospital. Look to my right and…

FATHER *does a movement… this could be something subtle, a gentle tap of his chest, perhaps, or the opposite and something more overt as a clear calling… in either case, it initiates* OLDER *to stand.*

My missus is there… holding my hand, which isn't a hand, but this… wet flipper thing…

OLDER (*voiced whisper*). It's going to be okay…

FATHER. I'm thinking what's going to be okay, also… sea horses don't have flippers?! Suddenly, a doctor walks in dressed like she's about to do surgery and I look down… and no word of a lie, laid out in front of me? Are my two black hairy legs just wide open! Not only am I baffed that they're wide open… but the top half of my body is still sea horse!!!!

OLDER. PUSH!!!

FATHER. What?!

OLDER. COME ON BABY PUSH!!

FATHER. HUH?!

OLDER. PUUUUUSHHHH!!!!!

FATHER. I turn from my missus, back to my hairy black legs and –

OLDER. PUUUUUSHHH!!

FATHER. I CAN'T!!!!

OLDER. PUUUUUSH!!

FATHER. YOU PUSH!!! – wait –

OLDER. PUUUUSHHHHHHH!!!!

FATHER. I'm PUSHING!!!!! – Wait something's…

OLDER. PUUUUUSH!!!!

FATHER. Something's coming out of me?!

OLDER. PUUUUUUSHHHH!!!

FATHER. My son's coming out of me?!

OLDER. PUUUUUUUUUUU –

FATHER. And I'm pushing and pushing and I'm baffled, but I'm pushing and this – he's – this small being slips out of me!! And he's crying his first cry and the doctor lifts him up, shows him to me and I see his face for the first time and she puts him in my arms **and everything just –**

> FATHER*'s body melts with joy, love and wholeness, the feeling of holding your child for the first time. It oozes out of him physically in slow motion. This moment takes him down to the floor, and as soon as he lays his body fully onto it, he shoots up – lights snap-change.*

> I'm back in bed… *my* bed, soaked with sweat, thinking… that was weird. Couldn't get back to sleep. It proper felt like he was coming out of me… and I started thinking, even though in real life he doesn't, he's still going to be *of* me, so he'd need to be moulded by me. I'd need to teach him everything I know – everything I stand for. At least, that's what I thought…

> SILENT MAN *approaches* FATHER. *They hold eye contact for a moment, then* SILENT MAN *takes a breath and begins the pulling motif towards* FATHER*'s chest. At the end of this,* SILENT MAN *seamlessly snaps into the movement*

FATHER *did when he held his baby for the first time. He tries to get* FATHER *to feel that feeling again.*

SILENT MAN *repeats the pulling motif into the soft movement over and over, but* FATHER *remains still, pain in his eyes. He denies this moment and walks back to his seat. As he does,* WISDOM *begins his motif, over the words 'I blame…' This is the first time* SILENT MAN *has not needed to do the personalised call to initiate the men to engage.* SILENT MAN *registers this new moment then walks back to his position.*

WISDOM *intercepts* FATHER *and directs the following dialogue to him.*

WISDOM. **I blame… I blame…** I blame the thinking!! Bruthas these days doing too much of it! Making life harder than it needs to be!

FATHER *strolls back to his seat, heavy.* WISDOM *turns to the audience.*

Life is simple! It's maths and science, left or right, stand or sit. You get an equation – work it out – move on! It's what our ancestors did! Instead, bruthas these days are lost in abstract thoughts! I learnt a long time ago that thinking… too much of it? Will get your ass into some serious situations, or, just… Make you swerve them altogether. (*Beat. Then, in a Bronx accent.*). You're only allowed three great women in your lifetime, they come along like the great fighters, once every ten years… *A Bronx Tale* – chaaa! Classic film!! My three done passed me by boy! I kept missing them, or… they missed me… 'Cause I was doing too much of this! (*Taps head.*) trying so hard not to… didn't ever want to jump ship, like he did, so… didn't get on it. Single and ready to mingle, going two decades strong! And it's better this way. Everything makes sense this way. Keep myself to myself!

FATHER *stands.*

FATHER. You keep everything to your… I just don't see how this can work.

WISDOM. I won't lie, the third one? Kinda stung. She was… I felt like I was --- I was at my bredrin's wedding last year,

Tolu… The way Nigerians take their weddings SERIOUS!
It's like three different ceremonies wrapped into one! But
throughout the dancing, the changing outfits, all the
commotion… They'd always have this moment together.
Sometimes it would last a second, sometimes ten. She would
just… look at him. But this look was… it was like this warm
blanket that only they could see, and she'd be covering him
with it… holding him with it, with just a look… That's some
type of love innit!!… That's why… **I blame** love!!
Everyone's got the word confused these days, *especially* the
black community! These days when you hear that word
people think: roses, rings, chocolates – naaah man! Love is a
verb, not a noun. It's about the double-D… and no, I'm not
talking… doing and duty. It's about what you do with your
hands… carrying – protecting – attacking… affection don't
pay the bills! Acts of service does. Waking your ass up at the
crack of dawn – providing – putting clothes on backs – no
slouching – sacrifice. Just like my grandad showed me. Being
a man and doing what you're supposed to, and if you're
doing it right, there ain't no space for any of that other stuff…

Beat. WISDOM *glances at his hands. A softness edges
through. Perhaps he briefly rubs them, remembering
something delicate they used to do. But almost as soon as this
moment happens, he throws it away and goes straight into –*

Yeah… I blame love.

SILENT MAN *approaches* WISDOM. *He starts the
beginnings of the pulling motif towards* WISDOM, *but then
stops himself. After a beat, he begins to soulfully sway his
head and shoulders, as if he's alone, listening to his favourite
piece of music. The movement is easy and warm.* WISDOM
*has a look in his eye, his body knows this feeling, this
movement, but he shrugs it off, gives* SILENT MAN *a
condescending look and walks back to his seat.*

SILENT MAN *sighs, then looks out to the audience. Spotlight.*

SILENT MAN *walks into it. He glares at the audience. Beat.*

*He then pulls his trousers down a bit lower and tries to look
'cool' – to look effortlessly like a 'brutha'. He plays about a
bit, trying to find the right stance and then…*

YOUNG BUCK *suddenly enters the spotlight…* SILENT
MAN *freezes: 'You're not supposed to be here?!'…*

YOUNG BUCK *gives* SILENT MAN *a Black Nod.* SILENT
MAN *takes it in, this is his chance to do what he's been
practising! After a beat, he gives* YOUNG BUCK *a nod
back, but… it looks slightly awkward and* SILENT MAN
knows it. Damn.

YOUNG BUCK *glances at him, confused, then looks out to
the audience. After a small beat,* SILENT MAN *also turns to
the audience, taking us into…*

'My Low Batty is Lower Than Yours'

They both look out to the audience.

After a beat, YOUNG BUCK *glances at* SILENT MAN, *then
back to the audience.*

SILENT MAN *glances at* YOUNG BUCK, *then back to the
audience.*

Beat.

YOUNG BUCK *glances at* SILENT MAN*'s trousers, then back
to the audience.*

After a beat, YOUNG BUCK *subtly pulls his tracksuit bottoms
a bit lower.*

Beat.

SILENT MAN *looks over at* YOUNG BUCK*'s tracksuit –
looks back up.*

Beat.

SILENT MAN *pulls his trousers ever so slightly lower than*
YOUNG BUCK*'s and…*

You get this gist!

This will build and build until, well… until YOUNG BUCK
*feels like he has no other choice but to pull his trousers ALL
THE WAY DOWN TO HIS ANKLES… revealing his polka-dot
boxers to the world.* YOUNG BUCK *looks out with a fat grin
that says 'There's no way you can top that!'… and he's right.*

SILENT MAN *shakes his head, and walks back to his position.*

YOUNG BUCK *begins his motif with 'You see me…', even
more cocky than usual.*

YOUNG BUCK. **You see me** yeah?! **You see me!…**

> YOUNG BUCK *stops, looks down, pulls his trousers back
> up and goes straight into –*
>
> You see me and dishes!? We don't get along. We got one of
> them hate-hate relationships.
>
> After I finish my food, I just wanna smash the plate. I'd
> rather smash it than have to clean it. Why's man cleaning
> dishes for?! So long! Gotta go downstairs, open the bin,
> brush the leftovers…
>
> YOUNG BUCK *physicalises the rest of the plate-washing in
> a slightly clownish manner.*
>
> …And there's always this *one* last little bump of food, that
> feels like someone's superglued it to the plate!!! LONG!

FATHER. You eat from it, you clean it! I ain't your slave!

YOUNG BUCK. Her favourite line. Man offered her a fair
swap! Sat her down and said 'Mum, if you clean my dishes
for me, I will go shopping for you… once every three
months.' (*Beat.*) Decent innit!? There was this one time, for a
whole week when I finished with the plate… I'd just tuck it
in a box behind the kitchen cupboard. She didn't know shit!
Until she did. Burst into my room and poured them all over
my bed, all mouldy and that! And I'm like, naaaaaah – threw
them off! That's when it got political –

FATHER. GET ON YOUR KNEES AND PICK THEM UP!

YOUNG BUCK. Dad never washed no plates, so why do I have
to?!

WISDOM. Man is built to be the breadwinner.

YOUNG BUCK. And that's exactly what I'm about! Getting that bread, and winning!... Boy, did she go up a decibel when I said that! So I turned my speakers on to drown out the high frequencies coming my way, and she stops, walks over... and yanks it onto the floor!! SPLIT IN HALF YA NA!!! – you're definitely paying for that!!

FATHER. I paid for it in the first place.

YOUNG BUCK (*goes to retort, then stops himself*). Couldn't really say anything back to that, so... just started smashing all the plates. I made sure every single one of them was MERKED!! She was going in!

FATHER. YOU GOT NO RESPECT!

YOUNG BUCK. I'm this – I'm that... I weren't really listening until –

FATHER. YOU'RE JUST LIKE YOUR DAD!!!

A very long beat.

YOUNG BUCK. And I looked at her. Then left, leaving a fist-sized dent in the wall on the way out. I started rolling the streets on one!! I was... inside it was like --- my thoughts were beefin each other and it was happening too fast for me to control – chest bare **tight –** hard to **breathe –** mad **headache –** I WAS VEX!! She can't be saying that. Man's here!! Get me – man's... I ain't run off – I ain't said I was only going away for a month and never come back. Ain't got some next yat pregnant... MAN'S ABOUT!!! And you're saying I'm like **him?!**

FATHER *sits.* OLDER *leans forwards, sees something familiar in* YOUNG BUCK. *He stands, watching* YOUNG BUCK *intently and slowly walks over as* YOUNG BUCK*'s breath and body continues to fill with rage.*

I was... I wanted to... I wanted to **EAT THE FUCKING WORLD!!** I wanted to tear everything apart and eat the fucking world!!!...

OLDER *tentatively approaches him.*

OLDER (*under his breath*). Let it go man… just let it go… let it
go…

> OLDER *is now opposite* YOUNG BUCK. *They begin a
> movement sequence…* OLDER *trying to quell* YOUNG
> BUCK – YOUNG BUCK *deflecting every attempt –*

Shit is poison, bro! It's burning you from the inside!…

> *The sequence crescendos with them on the floor in a grapple
> perhaps –* YOUNG BUCK *jolting like a caged animal,
> over…*

YOUNG BUCK. COME OFF ME!!!

> YOUNG BUCK *still jolts. Beat.*

> *Then –*

OLDER. WOULD YOU LET A BRUDDA COME INTO
YOUR YARD AND SHIT ON YOUR FLOOR???

> YOUNG BUCK *stops, glances at* OLDER: 'What the
> fuck?!'

WOULD YOU LET A BRUDDA COME INTO YOUR
YARD AND *SHIT* ON YOUR FLOOR?!

> *If they're in a grapple, they seamlessly release from it and
> stand.*

> *During below,* YOUNG BUCK *looks out to the audience,
> glued to his spot.* OLDER *perhaps slowly circles him. On the
> words in bold, sharp movements of rage and/or fear burst
> from* YOUNG BUCK.

But most importantly, you don't do anything. You don't
move. You just stand there, with this pile of shit right in front
of you, just stand there. Five minutes later, another guy
comes in and this brudda had curry the night before, so you
know what that means, innit? Then **BOOM!!** Woman bursts
in, white-girl wasted and projectile vomits all over the room
and there you are! Standing in this concoction of vomit and
shit, but you don't do anything, even though you know at
any point you can walk away, but you also know as soon as
you move, that smell will hit your nostrils ten times more so

you don't. You stand there. You stay in the **shhhh** – 'cause actually, it's not too bad. Yeah, you get a few waves of it that hit you every now and then, but if you don't move, if you stay still and look up, you can live with it, live *in* it. Just don't move. Look up and stand in your **shit**. 'Cause it's yours. It's in your house. Your body. Your pain and you just live with it, act from it 'cause it's easier that way, right?

Beat.

OLDER *returns to his chair. We see a shift in* YOUNG BUCK. *Lights change to their previous state.*

YOUNG BUCK. I get back home at like one a.m. See a plate on the table, wrapped in foil. Curry goat and rice… my favourite. Eat it, go bed. (*Beat.*) But I can't lie, I felt kinda weird leaving it… so I went down and cleaned my plate before I slept, still.

YOUNG BUCK *walks back to his seat.* SILENT MAN *intercepts him.* YOUNG BUCK *seems less stand-offish than before.* SILENT MAN *slowly raises his hand (as a gun) to* YOUNG BUCK*'s head.* YOUNG BUCK *does the same to* SILENT MAN.

Beat.

SILENT MAN *slowly pulls his hand away from* YOUNG BUCK *towards his own head, as if he's putting the 'gun' to it.* YOUNG BUCK *does the same… and just before the gun reaches their heads,* SILENT MAN *turns his hand sideways and slowly starts to shake it rhythmically.*

YOUNG BUCK *picks up the movement… we eventually realise that* SILENT MAN *and* YOUNG BUCK *are doing the beginnings of a 'gun-finger skank'.*

YOUNG BUCK *starts to really get into it, but then suddenly catches himself, throws the movement away and aggressively bops back to his seat.*

SILENT MAN *is left alone, now visibly weaker. He walks downstage-centre…*

Spotlight.

He walks into it, does a 'spud' towards the audience. Stops and goes again, and again… tries different angles and versions… spud with a thumb, sideways spud, Superman spud…, etc! But none of them feel or look right to him. He maybe bursts into a random dance with his spud out of pure frustration. He then goes into a 'hand slap brutha hug'. Again, tries different versions, but eventually gives up.

A long beat.

He then slowly begins to raise his arms into a kind of holding position. This looks and feels very different to his earlier attempts. He's not trying to perform anything, but still looks awkward and confused about how to do what he's trying to do.

He tries again and again, then shakes his head dismayed and…

SLAM!

DRUMMER *hits the drum –* SILENT MAN *swiftly moves across the stage. As he does,* WISDOM *peels into the space, opposite* SILENT MAN, *taking us into…*

'How the Fuck Do You Hug Another Brutha???'

SILENT MAN *continues trying to hold this invisible thing with great difficulty* (*the audience shouldn't know what he's trying to do until later*).

WISDOM *looks over at* SILENT MAN *for a beat, then looks out and decides to also try and do this thing. But like* SILENT MAN, *he can't seem to follow through with it fully. They both look and feel awkward as hell and their confusion builds with every attempt. As they change positions, they unknowingly get closer and closer to each other, until they eventually find themselves face to face – trying to do this awkward thing TO each other…*

Hug.

The physical awkwardness could be humorous at times, but the sequence should be rooted in the painful truth of these black men not knowing how to hug each other (without the masculine brutha handshake beforehand…)

With one final attempt, they manage to edge closer and closer, almost touching now – this moment will be drawn out as long as it needs to be. And JUST before they fully complete the hug, music swells and they IMMEDIATELY let go.

The rest of the ensemble spill into the space, briefly doing the same hugging motif and then leaving FATHER *onstage.*

FATHER. **I remember… I remember…**

I remember changing his first nappy. I remember thinking someone needs to invent some kind of self-cleaning nappy, 'cause it is no fun. I remember holding him for the first time… bliss. I think back to when I stopped holding him, as he got older. I'm thinking did I ever really *hold* him? Thinking back to how my dad held me, how he didn't hold me – but that's okay, 'cause I didn't need that. I remember my mum and dad, both present. No broken family – arguments, here and there, hard times? Goes without saying… but both there. But he… you can be there, in the flesh, but not actually be *there*.

I couldn't --- I wanted to --- but it felt like it wasn't allowed. Wasn't what happened in that space – and that's okay, 'cause I didn't need that. I remember him always saying –

WISDOM. My only job is to teach you to be a stand-up man.

FATHER. I remember my first fight –

OLDER *shoots up and looks over to* SILENT MAN.

OLDER. STAND UP MAN!!! STAND UP MAN!

SILENT MAN *reluctantly stands.* WISDOM *and* YOUNG BUCK *become 'hype men' for this playground fight.* OLDER *and* SILENT MAN *circle each other, amped up.*

FATHER. Fists clenched. Eyes targeted. And this uncontrollable rage ready to pour out and into him. I wanted to tear every inch of skin from his body and see his blood – his veins – his heart!!

OLDER *and* SILENT MAN *aggressively burst into each other, but as soon as they touch, an unexpected duet of softness begins. Builds and builds and crescendos with* OLDER *and* SILENT MAN *glaring at each other. Still.*

Beat.

I wanted to see his heart.

OLDER *stays in his position and watches as* SILENT MAN *walks over to* FATHER *and begins the movement motif – trying to pull something out of* FATHER*'s chest. And for the first time,* FATHER *accepts this moment and his chest jolts out.* SILENT MAN *then snaps into a soft movement (perhaps the movement* FATHER *did when holding his son for the first time).* FATHER *does this motif with him… he becomes emotionally affected.*

Music swells and the rest of the men peel into the space. And for the first time, we see a collective moment of physical softness between the men. Holds and lifts… eye contact and warmth.

The sequence crescendos leaving OLDER *onstage.*

OLDER. **I wanna feel… I wanna feel…**

FATHER (*Nigerian accent*). IF YOU DON'T HEAR, YOU WILL *FEEL*!!

OLDER. He edged closer, glasses off and glared at me with those eyes… the eyes every Nigerian son knows –

FATHER. EXPLAIN YOURSELF! COME ON!!!

OLDER. I had nothing! No words – just panic. And then… it began.

WISDOM *stands and approaches centre-stage.*

I'd always see it in slow motion, like he was a human transformer. Every physical shift and change igniting another…

OLDER *circles* WISDOM *as he begins to slowly physicalise the following.*

He takes up the stance, left leg forwards, right behind... Knees at a slight bend, giving him perfect support from the ground up... He tucks his bottom lip under his front teeth, as the layers of skin on his cheek pull back to create a grimace... His right arm simultaneously rises and extends into a perfect forty-five-degree angle, reaching the ideal point for highest speed and velocity... And then, well... he beat the *shit* out of me!

WISDOM *comes alive and begins to chase* OLDER *with his raised hand.* OLDER *runs for it, and the ensemble simultaneously shoot up from their seats and, in twos (one of them the 'father' the other the 'son'), chase each other around the space. This shouldn't be aggressive, more in the vein of a Tom and Jerry chase.* DRUMMER *underscores this moment.*

The ensemble eventually land back onto their chairs, apart from OLDER.

But it's just how it is innit! Chapter Three of the African rule book. Chapter One: Pride. Two: Read Your Book. Three?... Beats. Back in school days, me and my boys created the ABS... African Beating Society. We'd huddle up every lunch break and swap our latest chronicles with each other. But it's just our culture innit and discipline is an integral part of it. (*Beat.*) I was certain I'd do the same when I have a son, but... it's gotta go somewhere, all those beats – look at Black Panther! When he gets hit, he soaks up all the kinetic energy, keeps hold of every strike and when the time comes? Triples its output power! Forcing your hand onto another, especially your blood? Something must get passed over, then what?

SLAM!!!

DRUMMER *aggressively hits his drum.* OLDER *shifts his body and focus towards* DRUMMER. *He stays like this for the rest of the scene.*

I was upstairs in my room and kept hearing these...

SLAM – SLAM – SLAM!!

I shot out to find my older sister, with this helpless look on her face. Dad was over. He was downstairs with my younger sister doing maths homework. She was thirteen… fourteen, at the time, and her and maths were not friends –

FATHER. Six times seven, *is*???

OLDER. She answered – voice shaking with fear –

SLAM!!!

OLDER*'s body jolts, representing the vibration of the hit.*

Her screeches vibrated through the walls into our chests.

FATHER. SIX TIMES SEVEN IS??

OLDER. She plucked random numbers out of the air and –

SLAM! – OLDER jolts.

Forty-two, forty-two!! We kept repeating – hoping – praying the answer would somehow travel through the walls to her…

FATHER. WHAT. IS . SIX. TIMES . SEVEN???

A very long beat. DRUMMER *and* OLDER *lock eyes as* DRUMMER *slowly and threateningly lifts his hand, holds it above his head for a beat and –*

SLAM! SLAM! SLAM!

OLDER *suddenly bursts towards* DRUMMER, *now standing a few paces away from him.*

OLDER. STOP IT DAD, JUST STOP IT!!!! (*Beat.*) She leaped into my arms, shaking like a leaf. Her heart felt like it wanted to burst out of her chest and into mine. And there we were… Us on one side, him on the other. This weren't part of the rule book. We didn't know this land and neither did he. We were ready for him to just explode. But instead, he just glared at us with those eyes, as they flickered from rage, to fear, to confusion and then…

DRUMMER *starts to slowly look away.*

He started crying… he started crying.

Beat.

SILENT MAN *walks over to* OLDER. *He begins the pulling motif towards him and, for the first time,* OLDER *accepts it – his chest jolts out on every pull.* SILENT MAN *then snaps into a slow sensual movement with his chest and arms at the end of the pulling motif.* OLDER *denies it at first, but slowly allows it to infect him. They repeat the motif together and then* SILENT MAN *edges away, leaving* OLDER *alone as he continues the movement. Muffled sounds of some neo-soul music fades in... Jill Scott, Erykah Badu, Dwele... Something that gets* OLDER*'s body to organically move, boundless and free.*

But after a beat, he snaps out of it. Something stops him from reaching that full potential of joy and freedom... his pain. The music fades away. He saunters back to his seat.

WISDOM *suddenly shoots up, intercepts* OLDER *and directs the following to him.*

WISDOM. **I blame... I blame... I blame...** the discipline!!

WISDOM *turns to the audience.* OLDER *continues back to his seat, affected.*

Youts these days ain't got none! It starts from the home. That's the training ground! Discipline teaches you focus, strength, control – teaches you the power of a black man's hands! (*Beat, glares at his hands.*) **These hands... these hands** can whip up a storm in the kitchen ya na!!

OLDER. You sure you ain't got some Nigerian genes up in that DNA? 'Cause your jollof rice is OFF THE CHAAAIN!!!!

WISDOM. Official certification from my Nigerian bredrin! That's right, this Caribbean can make better jollof than nine out of ten Nigerians! And Ghanaians for that matter!! Wanna know the secret?... Ginger. Too many people forget the ginger! Just a likkle nub – it's what gives it that kick! Thai green curry, paella, carrot cake – I could do it all! Loved it man... making something beautiful from scratch with **these hands**. Wanted to be a chief – Michelin!... But he took me out of college to work in his construction business. Wanted me to use **these hands** for building, carrying, picking up dirt – for us, not them. He knew the odds of **these hands** becoming a chef, back then?... Boy!... but the black men around me *knew* what was good for me. Takes a village, you see?... Takes a village...

Takes a...

WISDOM *loses track of his thought, as he catches sight of his hands and gets lost in something. He starts to gently rub them and a delicate sequence of movement emerges, one that could explore the intricate nature of cooking and his love for it, then, perhaps, slips into the energy and feeling of him holding an invisible woman with adoration and softness, but after a few moments, something inside him begins to fight back. His hands snap into abrupt movement, full of resentment and aggression... Crescendos into –*

That's why I blame the village!! These youts ain't got one! Or if they have, the village ain't teaching them the proper way! Ain't taking control! Ain't directing them on how to use these hands! The village is teaching these youts to cook jollof without the ginger!!!! Yeah... I blame the village.

WISDOM *walks back to his seat.* SILENT MAN *intercepts him and begins the pulling motif towards* WISDOM*'s chest and then snaps straight into a soft body sway (unique to and for* WISDOM*).*

WISDOM *picks it up for a moment, closes his eyes and starts to really get into it. And we hear the muffled sounds of Bob Marley & The Wailer's 'Stir It Up' fade in, ever so slightly. But as quick as it arrives, is as quick as it goes.*

WISDOM *shoots his eyes open, replaces the softness back with stoicism and saunters off to his seat.*

Spotlight...

SILENT MAN *bops into it, then goes into a Black Nod, then a spud, then a brutha hug... taking us into...*

'Mirror Talk'

SILENT MAN *practises and performs all the different versions of 'black maleness' he explored earlier. But as he continues, things start to take a turn... the performance of this 'blackness' morphs into something toxic... the spuds, head nods and other moves merge into each other uncontrollably, creating a concoction of confusion, desolation and fear.*

The solo crescendos. SILENT MAN *is left breathless. He walks back to his position, dishevelled.*

YOUNG BUCK *shoots up.*

YOUNG BUCK. **You see me** yeah!... **You see me?!**

You see whenever I enter an English class? I always feel like I'm in a battlefield, just swerving these high-class word bullets! Teacher always tryna get man to speak like the Queen and dat!

FATHER. Act Three, Scene Two –

YOUNG BUCK. And what is it with this Shakespeare goon that gets people so horny man?!

FATHER. You've had a week to dissect the scene and importantly, the speech –

YOUNG BUCK. Do you know what would be mad?! If the Queen... (*Makes a circle with his left hand.*) Shakespeare... (*Lifts his right index finger, then penetrates the circle with it, multiple times.*) Baby would probs come out with a moustache and dat! Even the way it cries would sound posh... Waaaaa! Waaaaaa!

FATHER. I'm going to read the speech, go around the class and one by one in your own words, I want you to interpret –

YOUNG BUCK. Only plus about being in dry-ass English, was sitting next to sexy Serena. Been tryna break that in for five months! Slow burner, gotta make her laugh and that innit, so I'd always pass her these little –

FATHER *shoots into the space.*

FATHER. Come on! Pass it over...

YOUNG BUCK. Allow it man!

FATHER. I'm not going to ask you again.

> YOUNG BUCK *sulks, goes into his pocket and hands a piece of paper over to* WISDOM, *who reads it…*

Doth thou want to go out with man?…

So class, we have a treat! Seeing as Mr Lover Lover has got time to pass notes, he must know the speech inside out! Let's put it to the test.

YOUNG BUCK. Oh my days…

FATHER. Your days are going to get much longer, if you don't do this.

YOUNG BUCK. Come on sir!!!

FATHER. Lower your voice. Always have to be the loudest person in the room.

YOUNG BUCK (*under his breath*). Semi-professional…

FATHER. What's that?

YOUNG BUCK. I said let's go then innit!

FATHER. Right, here we are then. To be, or not to be, that is the question… go on…

YOUNG BUCK. Should… Should man be here, or… should man just, like, I dunno… dust innit!

FATHER. O-kay. Whether 'tis nobler in the mind to suffer the slings and arrows of outrageous fortune…

YOUNG BUCK. Is man on it enough to take all the madness of this life ting and just sit there like a prick –

FATHER. ERM!

YOUNG BUCK. Idiot…

FATHER. Or, to take arms against a sea of troubles and by opposing, end them…

YOUNG BUCK. Or, should man bring arms house against it all! BRRRRAAAPPPPPP!!

FATHER. To die – to sleep, no more…

A long beat.

YOUNG BUCK *starts to soften.*

YOUNG BUCK. All dying is, is sleeping anyway…

FATHER. And by a sleep to say we end the heartache and the thousand natural shocks –

YOUNG BUCK. That this life ting brings, always feeling like the loudest person in the room, even when I don't say a word… laying down and sleeping would make it all just stop. Who wouldn't want that?!

YOUNG BUCK *is affected. He suddenly loses his sense of gravity. The ensemble immediately run up to support him physically.* YOUNG BUCK *allows this support for a brief moment, then shuffles them off and stands back upright.*

But if all dying is, is sleeping and when you sleep you dream, then… oh, snap…

He loses his sense of gravity again. The men immediately support him, for a beat longer this time. YOUNG BUCK *shuffles them off.*

'Cause when man slips into that deep sleep, I don't know what's gonna come after it, don't know what dreams are gonna try come in and I ain't on that! Gotta be in control, *always.* And maybe that's why we force ourselves to stay awake in this world, this madness – even though a part of you wants to sleep so bad… so bad… so –

YOUNG BUCK *loses his sense of gravity, fully this time. The ensemble immediately support him and this builds into a movement sequence. The men try to physically become* YOUNG BUCK*'s sense of gravity. They try to keep him upright. This builds into lifts and holds.*

Sequence crescendos, leaving FATHER *holding* YOUNG BUCK.

Beat.

YOUNG BUCK *suddenly snaps back into his protective mode and shuffles away from* FATHER.

'Cause who would bear the whips and scorns of time, the oppressor's wrong, the white eyes drilling, the pigs stopping and searching, the voices starting and stopping, the box I tick in, the vex I spit out –

FATHER. When he himself might his quietus make –

YOUNG BUCK. AND JUST END IT!

A moment of stillness.

FATHER *then begins to approach* YOUNG BUCK.

The dialogue below should be played as two bruthas simply talking to each other, about something bruthas don't really talk about.

Who would bear to grunt and sweat a weary life…

FATHER. Unless, you weren't kinda scared of the things that could come after you sleep…

YOUNG BUCK. The undiscovered country…

FATHER. That where you go, you never return…

YOUNG BUCK. Puzzles the will…

FATHER. And you think about it all the time…

YOUNG BUCK. But never find answers…

FATHER. Just more questions…

YOUNG BUCK. And you feel kinda stuck –

FATHER. But somehow, you kinda choose to be –

YOUNG BUCK. 'Cause sleeping seems *so* easy –

FATHER. But *so* hard –

YOUNG BUCK. And you're lost between the easy and the hard and that makes you heavy, but you feel like you're floating.

Beat.

Wherever SILENT MAN *is, he goes over to* YOUNG BUCK *and begins the pulling motif towards* YOUNG BUCK*'s chest…*

YOUNG BUCK *accepts it – his chest erratically jolts out on every pull. He is left, weakened.*

Beat.

SILENT MAN *slowly raises his right hand (as a gun) to* YOUNG BUCK*'s head.* YOUNG BUCK *slowly does the same to* SILENT MAN.

Beat.

SILENT MAN *slowly pulls his hand away from* YOUNG BUCK *towards his own head, almost as if he's putting the 'gun' to it.* YOUNG BUCK *does the same and, just before the 'gun' reaches their heads,* SILENT MAN *turns it sideways and slowly starts to shake it rhythmically.* YOUNG BUCK *picks up the movement, the beginnings of a 'gun-finger skank'…*

Muffled sounds of grime music slowly fade in and, unlike before, YOUNG BUCK *accepts this moment and starts to psychically free himself into this skank…*

This builds and eventually the music blares out fully…

'Clash' by Dave, or something of the like. Either way, YOUNG BUCK *skanks like no one is watching!!!! Gun fingers galore, head bops wildly, arms shoot all over the place…he looks erratic, perhaps even 'aggressive' to some, but it's his freedom, his release, his joy.*

This builds and builds…

Then, after a beat, the music becomes muffled again and goes into slow motion. YOUNG BUCK*'s movement simultaneously goes into slow motion with it, as* FATHER *enters* YOUNG BUCK*'s light and circles him, eyeing him intently. The music fades away, but* YOUNG BUCK *still moves in slow motion.*

FATHER. **I remember… I remember…**

I remember his tenth birthday, the light in his eyes as he danced. 'Smooth Criminal' on repeat and him in the centre, looking like the Tasmanian devil! Arms and legs flying all over the place! So much light in his eyes... then I remember the week after, sitting him down and giving him the talk...

YOUNG BUCK *snaps out of his movement and stands still.*

The one before the birds and the bees –

Blackout.

We stay in black over the following dialogue, which happens as a voice-over. The sound of FATHER*'s voice could bounce from the speakers on the left, to the speakers on the right, during different lines... simulating the feeling of black boy's having to juggle all this information in their minds.*

(*Voice-over.*) As soon as you step out of this house, you will be aware at all times. Your centre of gravity will shift depending on the room you enter. You will be invisible, yet hyper-visible. You will give space and unconsciously create it. You will walk down the street and you will not have right of way. Your heart will change pace as your walking does. You'll soften your voice, lower your chin and smile when you don't really want to.

You're three-sixty, you're whole, you're more than one thing – but when you're in a tracksuit and hoody?... You are only one thing. You will sweat and sweat, you will think ahead and you will plan accordingly. You will be the exception to the rule, be doubted, receive double looks... and at times you will think it's all in your head. You will hold it all and it will repeat. Day in, day out... and you will have to keep going.

Beat.

Lights snap back on.

SILENT MAN *is centre-stage looking over to* FATHER, *who is now downstage-right, on one knee. As if he's just given the talk to his son. He takes a heavy breath and stands. Starts off to his seat.*

SILENT MAN *intercepts him. He begins the pulling motif towards* FATHER*'s chest, and, this time,* FATHER *accepts it.*

His chest jolts out on every pull. SILENT MAN *pulls and pulls and, on the last one, the velocity of it takes* FATHER *from his position back to his seat.*

Beat.

A breathless SILENT MAN *looks out to the audience...*

Beat.

No spotlight...

Instead, SILENT MAN *walks forwards and lands in the position he normally does. But perhaps, this time, he simply just looks out to the audience. Perhaps, this time, he doesn't 'perform' anything... just looks at them, breaking the wall of the mirror. And maybe he smiles. And maybe that smile turns into a warm laugh. Whatever happens here, we just stay with* SILENT MAN... *this black man, standing in the space, as him and just being. A simple yet, at times, radical act.*

After a long beat of this, SILENT MAN *walks back to his position.*

WISDOM *shoots up.*

WISDOM. **I blame... I blame...** I blame the weather!!! Chaaa! It's too cold man! If this year's summer was a title of a film, it would be: *Gone in 60 Seconds...* – blinked and it was over!!

OLDER. WELL GO BACK TO YOUR OWN COUNTRY THEN!!!

On the above line, and OLDER*'s subsequent lines,* WISDOM *could perhaps do a movement that represents his true inner fear of that moment, then snaps out of it as soon as the line ends.*

WISDOM. I'm gonna get a T-shirt with that printed on, just for the banter! 'Cause every brother and sister of my generation remembers the first time someone told them that. I was sixteen, washing my grandad's windows, bopping my head, shoulders, knees and toes to some Bob Marley of course... and this old white fella, with his thick square glasses, bushy eyebrows and pot belly probably full of baked beans and

unseasoned chicken… bowls up out of nowhere, yanks my
Walkman from the seal and –

OLDER. GO BACK TO YOUR OWN – !

WISDOM. I was shocked! Took me three months to save up for
that Walkman! And… I was in a moment. The music was --- I
was in a moment, you know? And he took that away from me.
But you know what? The older I got, the more I realised… he
was completely right. All of them are. This country ain't mine!
Never has been! Not really. If we ain't getting the –

OLDER. GO BACK! –

WISDOM. Then we're getting the wide eyes and bright smile
that underneath, say the same thing. So why stay!? What,
human right?!… Well, it's my human right to know when to
say enough is enough. (*Beat.*) What if…

WISDOM *looks back to the row of men, seated.*

All of us, every single black person in England packed up
and gweh!!!…

The men stand and walk towards WISDOM.

Granted, they would have to get past their whole economy
going to shit… But can you imagine it? If we just moved on
– made our own – Malcom X'd the ting… Maybe it would
allow me to… allow us to…

FATHER, YOUNG BUCK *and* OLDER *are now stood
adjacent to* WISDOM, *looking directly at the audience. They
all take a deep and meaningful collective breath in and out.*
WISDOM *does a movement on each breath and over the
subsequent ones.*

Not a forced one…

The men take a deep breath in.

Not a fake one…

And a breath out.

One I think about changing…

Breath in.

One I have to control…

And out.

Not one I can't –

The men take another deep breath in. As above, WISDOM *simultaneously does a movement on the breath, but this time, he doesn't let it go. He holds on to his movement, tight. And so do all of the men, who now hold their breath.*

Beat.

YOUNG BUCK *looks over to* WISDOM, *then back to the audience.*

Beat.

More of the men look at WISDOM, *a slight sense of panic in their eyes and body… they're starting to suffocate. But* WISDOM *doesn't let go of his movement, his tight fists – which would allow the men to breathe again. Instead,* WISDOM *just glares at them, then looks back to the audience.*

Beat.

FATHER *loses his balance, starts to really struggle. Beat.*

YOUNG BUCK *drops to the floor.* SILENT MAN *stands. He wants to intervene, but doesn't know if he should.*

Beat.

More struggle and panic from the men. SILENT MAN *edges closer, conflicted.*

Beat.

And just before it looks like the men are about to collapse… WISDOM *lets go of his movement and the men immediately release their breath. They pant and take fast gulps of air.*

Beat.

It's crazy how the simple act of breathing has become political. (*Beat.*) That's why **I blame** the white man! Aka the weaponsier! This was a planned attack! Black-on-black crime… Absent black fathers… They take a fraction of truth, conflate it into a narrative, twist it into a noose and make you put it round your own neck! Our. Necks!! And I'm tryna make you wake up and see! Tryna make everyone see! But you all wanna stay asleep...

FATHER, OLDER *and* YOUNG BUCK *walk back to their seats, slightly dishevelled. They all sit, apart from* OLDER... *something stops him.*

That's why **I blame... I blame... I blame** the black man!!! The black man's got his head down, eyes closed, keeping his wins to himself! Crabs-in-a-bucket mentality! The black man needs to wake up and see how soft racism really is!! And if racism is soft? The black man has to be strong. Fists tight – back straight!

OLDER. But...

WISDOM *turns to* OLDER.

The ensemble look at each other and SILENT MAN, *slightly confused... the rules of this world seem to be crumbling.*

WISDOM. But what?!

OLDER *approaches* WISDOM.

OLDER. It's hard to keep your back straight when it feels like the world is on it.

WISDOM *laughs and looks back to audience.*

My grandad used to say, 'You have to learn to dance between the raindrops.' (*Points to* OLDER.) But the black man has forgotten how to dance! Too busy doing exactly what the white man planned!

OLDER *is now up-close to* WISDOM. *A duet emerges, perhaps* OLDER *tries to make* WISDOM's *back soften, but* WISDOM *wants to be firm and rigid – keeps shrugging* OLDER *off.*

It must be sore by now...

WISDOM. Got more chances than my generation ever had to be great! –

OLDER. It's okay to loosen it –

WISDOM. To live a better life! Instead they're doing chupidness on road or complaining about the so-called 'struggle'! Struggle ya na! You lot don't know no struggle!! Back then it was 'Go back to your own country!' Today, you got white people rocking dreads! Back then, it was 'Why is your food so weird and funny?', today you got Jamie Oliver making his 'punchy' jerk rice! Black is *in* now! Yeah, you might get a few things that crop up here and there, but ain't nowhere near like it was! The black man's coming like a loaf of freshly baked bread, without the crust! Just soft! Soaking everything up, letting it all in – no protection!!

OLDER. What are you protecting?

WISDOM. Yeah… I blame the black man.

WISDOM *walks back and sits.*

OLDER. **What are you protecting?… What are you protecting?**

Beat.

WISDOM *looks around at the men, then the audience, and then* SILENT MAN.

A long beat, then…

WISDOM. You know what? This is… I'm done.

WISDOM *bolts off.*

OLDER. **What are you protecting?…**

WISDOM *reaches the inner threshold of soil and… SLAM!!*

DRUMMER *hits the drum and* WISDOM *simultaneously hits an invisible barrier. He tries again…*

SLAM!!

SILENT MAN *stands to intervene, but* OLDER *shakes his head at him.* SILENT MAN *registers this new moment, then sits back down.*

WISDOM *keeps trying to leave. Gets more and more flustered.* OLDER *runs off, lifts some soil from the outskirts and approaches* WISDOM *with it.*

What are you protecting???

WISDOM *continues trying to leave with even more vigour.*

What are you protecting?!… What are you protecting?!!… What are you pro–

WISDOM. *EVERYTHING!!!!!!!*

A long beat.

WISDOM *turns to* OLDER.

OLDER *reaches over to* WISDOM *with his fist full of soil.*

OLDER. You need this…

Beat.

WISDOM *takes the soil into his hands, then slowly lets it slip through his fingers. He drops whatever is left, then looks at his hand, now empty.*

WISDOM. I don't need anyone.

OLDER *runs off, gets another fist of soil, runs back to* WISDOM *with it.* WISDOM *swipes it away, again and again – this builds into a movement sequence…*

OLDER *trying to get* WISDOM *to stay and soften,* WISDOM *wanting the opposite.*

The sequence crescendos with OLDER *seeming to have got through to him, well, enough to stop him leaving.*

OLDER *glances at* SILENT MAN *to take over, then returns back to his seat, leaving a worn-down* WISDOM.

SILENT MAN *walks over to* WISDOM *and begins the pulling motif,* WISDOM*'s chest jolts out on every pull.*

Beat.

SILENT MAN *slowly begins to sway his head.* WISDOM *catches onto this movement and, importantly, the feeling – it becomes his. He sways his head and shoulders, closes his eyes and starts to really get into it.*

SILENT MAN *walks back to his position.*

Lights focus on WISDOM *and the muffled sounds of 'Stir It Up' creep in, gradually becoming less and less muffled…* WISDOM *starts to really get in tune with his inner freedom – starts to move however the fuck he wants… his torso swirls, his arms peel through the space, he smiles, he laughs, maybe he even cries, but a cry rooted in joy and freedom.*

'Stir It Up' cross-fades with a swell of music, some heartfelt strings perhaps… and lights fade up to find YOUNG BUCK, OLDER *and* FATHER *spread around the space, perhaps in their own spotlights. And they're all moving in slow motion as if listening to their favourite piece of music. This will be unique to each of them and also echoed in how they each move. As referenced earlier,* YOUNG BUCK *could be listening to some grime – gun fingers galore…* OLDER *could be swaying to some soul,* FATHER *to some Afrobeat and so on… Whatever it is, they're in their own worlds, deeply connected and free.*

DRUMMER *hits his drum over the music and the men suddenly peel off their spots and join together, centre-stage.* SILENT MAN *joins them too and they continue on in what was first an individual moment of physicalised joy, into a collective one.*

Beat.

The music fades down… the men's movement slowly does too.

A long beat.

The men begin to look at each other, in a way they haven't before, then sit in a semicircle on the floor. SILENT MAN *joins them. The energy feels different now. Like a group of brothers sitting around a campfire. Ready and willing.*

FATHER *stands and directs the following to the men.*

FATHER. **I remember… I remember…** I remember asking him at the end of the film… 'Who's your favourite character?' Secretly wanting him to say Simba. King of the jungle innit! His land! His world! Power, respect, Simba… SIIIIIIIMBAAAA!!! (*Beat.*) Rafiki… (*Kisses teeth.*) Of all the characters to choose from, he goes for the baboon with the swollen ass, talking nonsense!! Rafiki ya na! I'd say 'Why not Simba? You should choose the lion!… You should choose the lion.' (*Beat.*) I used to think my job as a father was so many things. Teach him right from wrong, teach him –

WISDOM. Discipline.

OLDER. Strength.

FATHER. Honesty – qualities of a stand-up man. Qualities my father taught me, and his father's father, and his and his…

OLDER. And on and on –

FATHER. And yeah, they're important, but when I remember that moment, that scene… The iconic opening, when Rafiki marks Simba's forehead with the roots, goes to the highest ledge in the jungle and lifts him up, for the world to see. (*Sings.*) 'THE CIRCLE OF LIIIIIIIIFE!!!' (*Beat.*) Maybe that's all we're supposed to do. Just lift them up. To show him the world, but let him know he needs to live in it, create in it, make mistakes in it – to lift him up, but not forget to look into his eyes, to listen… let him fall, taste failure, find his way back to his feet, then lift him up again. Keep lifting and lifting, until he's too heavy to be lifted, and by that point, he's standing tall… ready to do the lifting. What if we all did that? What if the world ended, and we started again with just lifting? 'Cause I don't think I did… not high enough. If I did, I wouldn't have had to put him in the… A father ain't supposed to do that. And I'm left with this… **heaviness…** *we're* left with this **heaviness…** and it just waves over you – through you – shakes the fabric of your --- and when you think it's gone? When you forget – when you laugh, the memories slip back in and you're falling again --- you're falling --- you're ---

He stops and turns away, unable to continue – the pain is too much.

Beat.

FATHER *turns back.* SILENT MAN *catches his eye and nods at him, as if to say: 'You can do this'…* FATHER *tries again.*

'Cause I remember --- I remember ---

His inner turmoil takes him off the spot, as his pain bursts out of him uncontrollably... The weight. The fear. The grief.

Builds and builds – crescendos into –

I REMEMBER EVERYTHING!!! And I wish I had a second chance. I just want a second chance.

SILENT MAN rises. He goes over to FATHER and begins the pulling motif. FATHER fully accepts it. His chest shoots out, accompanied by his guttural breath sounds on each of SILENT MAN's pulls.

FATHER stands, breathless. He looks over to YOUNG BUCK.

Beat.

YOUNG BUCK stands and FATHER sits. YOUNG BUCK directs the following to the men.

YOUNG BUCK. **You see me** yeah!! **You see me! You see...**

I can't man...

YOUNG BUCK steps back – shakes his head over and over.

FATHER. When you look into my eyes, what do you see?

Beat.

YOUNG BUCK. What?

FATHER stands. Approaches YOUNG BUCK.

FATHER. Do you see?

YOUNG BUCK. Eyes?...

FATHER. Just eyes?

YOUNG BUCK. Brown eyes.

FATHER. What else?

YOUNG BUCK. I see your eyes and they're brown innit!

FATHER. You got two small brown dots in the white part, only in your left though – what else?

YOUNG BUCK. Fam! I see your eyes – they're brown – and... rahhh, your eyelashes are bare long you know!

They slip into a duet, seamlessly returning back to their face-to-face position.

FATHER. You got four curved lines beneath your lower eyelid. They join together in the corner –

YOUNG BUCK. Your pupil things are bare sharp too! And you got some mad streaks in the centre! Mad colours, like the rainbow and that!

Duet continues, then stops over –

FATHER. What else?

YOUNG BUCK. What?

FATHER. Else?

YOUNG BUCK. Nah, fam – this is… ain't ever looked in a brudda's eyes this long without it seeming –

FATHER. Soft?… You got a hard face, but soft eyes. What else?

YOUNG BUCK. I see your eyes – they're brown – got some long lashes – piercing pupils – mad streaks in the centre, like the colours of the rainbow… like the colors of the… colours of the…

Beat. Something clicks in YOUNG BUCK.

FATHER. Keep going…

FATHER *steps back, leaving* YOUNG BUCK *to his moment.*

YOUNG BUCK. I see it all inside of you – every colour inside of me, but they're fighting each other for space… I'm fighting you, myself and I for space – so when I look at you – when you look at me – when our eyes connect? I have to protect. To hold on to something, 'cause there's too much to feel! There's so many colours, but when you mix them all together you end up with black, the only one *they* see – *I* see – *you* see – but I got *all* of them in me! You see… **you see me**, yeah? Oi, Mr Ogun, **you see me!** – Oi, pigs, **you see me!** – Oi, parliament, **you see me!?** – Scared white lady, **you see me**?! – Security guard, **you see me!!** – DAD **YOU SEE ME?!?** – WORLD, **YOU SEE ME?!!?**

YOUNG BUCK*'s movement spills into space – builds and builds – crescendos into –*

DO YOU SEE ME?… DO YOU SEE ME?

Beat.

SILENT MAN *stands, about to walk over to* YOUNG BUCK, *but* FATHER *shoots up and takes over. He approaches* YOUNG BUCK, *looks at him for a beat, then begins the pulling motif towards his chest.* YOUNG BUCK *fully accepts it. His chest shoots out, accompanied by guttural breath sounds on each of* FATHER*'s pulls.*

Beat.

OLDER *and* YOUNG BUCK *sit.*

OLDER *stands.*

OLDER. **I wanna feel… I wanna feel… I wanna feel** like it's all tied up. Like one of them murder-mystery films where halfway through no one knows what the hell is going on, or who did what, but somehow –

YOUNG BUCK. It all ties up –

OLDER. But it's like you're walking with your laces undone, and you don't know how it happened, so you stop, tie them up – but two seconds later they're undone again. So you stop –

YOUNG BUCK. Tie them up.

OLDER. Stop –

YOUNG BUCK. Tie them up –

OLDER. But it keeps happening, so next time, you just leave it. You trip over every now and then, but after a while, the tripping becomes normal. You style it out. Act like you meant to trip – turn that trip into a bop – bouncing your soul aggressively off the concrete like you know exactly where you're going, but you're lost… and none of us are comparing notes! No one's giving me directions to that feeling and I wanna *feel* it man, I wanna feel it so in nine months' time I can pass it down to him so *he* can feel it too – **I wanna feel… I wanna feel… I wanna feel…**

*His movement builds, perhaps using the motif of tripping…
tripping over obstacles of a system stacked against him, one
that he feels has started to define him, and he tries to find his
way through… builds and builds – crescendos into –*

I WANNA FEEL JOY!!! Now and forever. I want to feel joy.

Beat.

The ensemble stands. Resolute in this collective need.

YOUNG BUCK *approaches* OLDER *and begins the pulling
motif.* OLDER *fully accepts it. His chest shoots out,
accompanied by guttural breath sounds on each of* YOUNG
BUCK'*s pulls.*

OLDER *glances at* WISDOM. *He reluctantly rises and
directs the below dialogue directly to the men.*

WISDOM. **I blame… I blame… I blame… I blame… I
blame…**

WISDOM *shifts between the men, as if placing the 'blame'
onto each of them. But after a beat, something opens up in
him and begins to take over… a need. His pain spills out
physically…*

Builds and builds – crescendos into –

I blame myself.

OLDER *approaches* WISDOM. *He begins the pulling motif.*
WISDOM *fully accepts it. His chest shoots out,
accompanied by guttural breath sounds on each of* OLDER'*s
pulls.*

Beat.

SILENT MAN *turns to the audience.*

*He begins the same physical motif he did in the prologue.
Repeats it over and over, but the energy of it seems different
now. Seems like less of a calling and more of a releasing…*

*As this happens, the ensemble grab fists full of soil and pace
around, psyching themselves up for something (like* SILENT
MAN *was in the prologue…)*

WISDOM *suddenly stops in front of* SILENT MAN, *touches his shoulder.* SILENT MAN *stops.* WISDOM *then begins doing the pulling motif towards* SILENT MAN*'s chest.*

SILENT MAN *seems confused at first, but accepts it. His chest shoots out, accompanied by guttural breath sounds on each of* WISDOM*'s pulls...*

WISDOM *steps back and* SILENT MAN *continues with his guttural breath sound. It now becomes rhythmic and, perhaps, slightly voiced. This moment will be the first time we hear* SILENT MAN*'s voice... and they aren't words... just a guttural sound of release.*

Lights fade up and...

The ritual begins... The full purging of their pain.

This will be a visceral, emotional release, rooted in the guttural release of the men's breath and a simple physical and rhythmic movement motif. This will peel around the space and burst into individual moments at times, but will always come back to them, together in this moment.

The soil should be used throughout this, perhaps as a vehicle for the men to break into moments of physical care, as the purging takes its toll on each of them.

This purging builds and builds...

And as it does, DRUMMER *stands and enters the playing space for the first time as the purging now morphs into celebration. The men peel around* DRUMMER *as he plays.*

Builds and builds...

Seems like it's just about to reach a crescendo, like we're about to end and...

Blackout.

But...

Epilogue

…the vocal sound of the men releasing together continues…

All the audience sees *is BLACK… yet, what they* hear *is an outpour of JOY, FREEDOM and RELEASE.*

This will go on…

And on…

And on…

And on…

And on…

And on…

And eventually simmer down to us being left with our final sound…

Six black men

breathing together

with openness and renewed strength…

The End.

A Nick Hern Book

Samskara first published in Great Britain in 2021 as a paperback original by Nick Hern Books Limited, The Glasshouse, 49a Goldhawk Road, London W12 8QP, in association with The Yard Theatre, London

Samskara copyright © 2021 Lanre Malaolu

Lanre Malaolu has asserted their moral right to be identified as the author of this work

Cover image: Guy J Sanders

Designed and typeset by Nick Hern Books, London
Printed in the UK by Mimeo Ltd, Huntingdon, Cambridgeshire PE29 6XX

A CIP catalogue record for this book is available from the British Library

ISBN 978 1 83904 059 7

Woodland
CARBON
www.woodlandcarbon.co.uk
NICK HERN BOOKS
Printed on Carbon Captured paper

www.nickhernbooks.co.uk

facebook.com/nickhernbooks

twitter.com/nickhernbooks